VOICES IN THE WIND

poetry today

Voices In The Wind

Edited by
Rebecca Mee

First published in Great Britain in 1998 by Poetry
Today, an imprint of
Penhaligon Page Ltd, 12 Godric Square, Maxwell Road,
Peterborough. PE2 7JJ

© Copyright Contributors 1998

All rights reserved. No part of this publication may be
reproduced, stored in a retrieval system, or transmitted
in any form or by any means, without prior permission
from the author(s).

A Catalogue record for this book is available from the
British Library

ISBN 1 86226 540 2

Typesetting and layout, Penhaligon Page Ltd, England
Printed and bound by Forward Press Ltd, England

Foreword

Voices In The Wind is a compilation of poetry, featuring some of our finest poets. The book gives an insight into the essence of modern living and deals with the reality of life today. We think we have created an anthology with a universal appeal.

There are many technical aspects to the writing of poetry and *Voices In The Wind* contains free verse and examples of more structured work from a wealth of talented poets.

Poetry is a coat of many colours. Today's poets write in a limitless array of styles: traditional rhyming poetry is as alive and kicking today as modern free-verse. Language ranges from easily accessible to intricate and elusive.

Poems have a lot to offer in our fast-paced 'instant' world. Reading poems gives us an opportunity to sit back and explore ourselves and the world around us.

Contents

The Choking Ticket Diminishing Authenticity	Deborah Johnston	1
Untitled	Pettr Manson-Herrod	2
12/12/95	Nicola Louise	3
Maybe	Nicola Lebish	4
Sunbathing	D Paulson	5
Irish Dream	Hazel E Henshaw	6
The Man From The Sea	Bessie	7
My Friend	E Woods	9
Let's Talk About Weston	Vee Smith	10
Possession	S L Cavers	12
Reprieve	C W Foord	14
The Old Chalice	Eric Ashwell	16
A Fabulous Pirate	S Taylor	18
The Cotton Fields	Diego Martinez-Montano	19
Withered Ramblings	A Weaver	20
To Catch A Star	G Cubitt	21
Thread Bear	John Christopher	22
Men Of War	Saiqa Hussain	23
Ocean	L King	24
Trend	G Cox	25
Zodiac	J Reeve	26
Paint Work	D Payn Le Sueur Warner	27
A Grain Of Light	Richard Cassidy	29
Evening	Carrie Snow	30
First Snow Of Winter	Janis Robertson	31
Rehearsal	Angela Wellings	32
Time Peace	Geoff Durham	33
Listening To Landini	Brian Stevens	34
Audition Dance	M Whitecross	35
From London To Liverpool	Michellejoy Hughes	36
Animal Adventure	Hazel Houldey	38
The Stones	Victoria Helen Turner	39
Dream	A R Frape	41
Acronychal Gloom	Alasdair Maciver	42

My Magnolia Bush	Ruth Kennedy	43
It's All In The Game	P D Hollington	44
The Unicorn	J E Alban	45
Jesus Was . . .	R C Thompson	46
One From The Heart	Debbie Boyt	48
The Sea	Christine M Matthews	49
The Hands Of Time	P Harvi	50
Unwritten Rules	P Larner	51
Angling Comrades	Peter Edward Waines Briggs	52
Waiting For The Man	Nic Miller	53
The Desert Song	Terri Fisher	54
Patient In Mental Home In Travnik	Audrey Lay	55
The Humble Rose	H R Jones	56
I Think Not Neigh, Astray Stay	Anita Branagan	57
Fat Fool	D A Seabright	58
Love, God, Father Xmas And The Tooth Fairy	Stephen Dulson	59
The Witch's Spell	Duncan Cook	60
Little Witch	Trudy Pickering	62
Verduna	Paul Butters	63
Fright	Adrian Vale	64
Bluebell Wood	Margaret Dominey	66
Merriment And Mirth	Stephen L Rogers	67
In Praise Of Gorse	Mary Ryder	68
Say Cheese!	Tracy Heaton	69
Something!	D Gregson	70
Blind	Andrea Smith	72
Technology	Irene Sutherland	74
In Praise Of Books	David Dillon	76
Ten Words	James Leonard Clough	77
The Irish Jig	A Gillmeister	79
A Stone's Throw	Ruth Watts	80
Machine Metal And Man	Vera Oxley	81
Fairies In Summer	Luke Daniel Gruber Prince	83
Black Night	Ananka Lyall	84
Sequence	Ann Easton	85
The Other Word	Anthony John Ward	87

The Barrel	Tim Davis	88
The Bookshelves Of Time	Alfred Tubb	89
Miscarried	Thelma Paolozzi	90
The Train Is Running Late	G Carpenter	91
Morning Call	Margaret Phillips	92
The Hero	Hazel Houston Hewitt	93
Diamond	Jan Duncan	95
Lost	Emily Victoria Hughes	97
The Heart Of The Matter	Elizabeth Mitchell	98
Voyage To Æaea	Bernard Brown	99
Consolation Prizes	E Kathleen Jones	100
Elevenses And All That	Fredk A Hays	101
Those Little Fruit	David J Pratt	102
Solo	Marian J Prebble	103
Hallowe'en	Becky Cole	104
A Shot In The Dark	Jeanette Latta	105

The Choking Ticket Diminishing Authenticity

We're told to hate the prickly bush,
The wicked weed,
Avoid it, scorn it, ignore it.
No good can come of pain.

Underneath a glimmer, a lovely glow,
Sometimes I see a wondrous rose,
A ray of hope, a warming smile.
As summer dawns, a magic moment.

It only takes a sprinkle, a tinkle of rain,
To close the flower and darken its name.
A brattle of thunder, its not even there.
For gone is the flower and up springs the thorn.

Clouds swallows the dim warmth, yet there is a light
Back to a war of briar and thicket.
For I've glimpsed a wonderful thing,
Its not often I see it, I cry,
I need it.

Deborah Johnston

Untitled

Little treasure,
Little beauty-
What is held in store for you?
April love may have seemed folly
As the last year followed through.

Now a January joy
Has brought you,
Beautiful into such love
As will be with you for ever.
May life touch you
With a golden glove.

Pettr Manson-Herrod

12/12/95

I lie alone. Remembering the days when life was easy and fun. Remembering the times when I never wanted the days to end . Now the world had changed with everything in it.

I thought that you were the one. My dreams had come true but the reality was to strong. What I would have given to see my dream through. Instead I saw a nightmare.

Now the memories are all I have left. Never has a power been so closely guarded than that of my love for you. Happiness is all I remember, Living a dream that can't come true.

Nicola Louise

Maybe

Have you ever thought.
What it would be like.
To go up in the sky.
And see the black of night?
To be up with the stars,
Float without gravity.
To be able to shout
And keep your sanity.
With wonders of the world,
Below you, so far down.
When you reach great heights,
Yet hear the smallest sound.
To find out about the veil
That covers the world at night.
To hold it in your fingertips
And have it in your sight!
You would wander on forever
Passing planets or a star
That seem when you're on Earth,
Up high, away so very far!

I think it would be best
To stay down here and see,
To stop wondering at things
That might or might not be!

Nicola Lebish

Sunbathing

Threatening clouds, across the sky,
Tried to deny my love and I,
Until our beds, to sheltered nook,
With books and radio, we took.

The warmth denied by blustery breeze,
Played on us now, through swaying trees,
So chatter died, and sleep ensued,
As warmth affected calmer mood.

A noisy bee, finding our hollow,
Decided then to quickly follow,
His constant buzz disturbed our rest,
Retreating fast, we left our nest.

D Paulson

Irish Dream

The haunting Irish music plays,
The dancers click their feet on stage,
The floor boards bounce and spring.
With the constant dancing,
And the shoes clicking.
The fiddlers play a lively jig.
While the dancers hop around the floor so big,
Now the drummers play their tune.
Male dancers have there turn.
The bagpipes' haunting sound.
Ring all around.
Causing an exhilarating sound.
It makes you think of lake and streams,
Of mystic moors, a captivating dream,
Oh for peace and quiet.
The music makes you so desire.
The guitars softly playing.
Dancers swaying.
Like flowers in the summer sun.
Young voices in the choir sing,
High pitched like little sparrows.
Bouncing around the sky like arrows.
Tears fall down my face.
As I allow the music to embrace.
The music so moving.
I too feel my feet roving.
The pipers play a tune of love.
The wild geese fly above.
Mystical music haunting.
The dancing fascinating.

Hazel E Henshaw

The Man From The Sea

The wind blew hard from farthest Labrador
and fell upon the tempest furrowed shore.
This winter's night in December 1792
a ship was lost with all the crew.

A lone survivor braved this storm
naked as the day he was born.
He climbed the cliff to where some wreckers stood,
going straight to a woman, who to him looked good.

From off her back, he took her cloak
to save his embarrassment to use as a coat.
With a flourish he jumped on the horse's back
arms round the woman, he gave the horse a slap.

They sped away to Galsham farm
to her father's house, away from harm
Her father welcomed him to their home
and bade he treat it like his own.

The woman Ann knew who this man would be
so they courted and got wed, August 1793.
Daniel Coppinger was his name
very soon for all wrecks he got the blame.

He'd lure them ashore with lamps on cattle
then watched the vessels with sea and rock battle.
If ashore came survivors, they were soon dead,
for Coppinger would smash in their head.

Red would be both sea and pool
while blood would drip from his killing tool.
Then plundering ship for food and store,
he took what he wanted in this bloody furore.

For years he terrorised this country fair,
murder, deception all evil was there.
Then came one stormy, windswept night:
time for Coppinger to take flight.

Customs and excise were on his tail,
they'd catch him this time, they couldn't fail.
From this shore he escaped on a brigantine
and from that day forth was never seen.

His wife, poor Ann, he left at home;
she died years later, all alone.
Around these parts, there is a rhyme
that they believe comes from this time:

If you save a man from the sea
he'll become your enemy.

    Bessie

My Friend

It seems like only yesterday
Since first I met my friend.
A solid, strong and sturdy girl
Her feet well on the ground.
Yet the time we've spent together,
She hardly makes a sound.
Yes, she hardly makes a sound.

A comfortable seat, she rides well,
Though brooks on interference.
Simple and easy to control,
Yet never leaving me alone,
On the journey's we've spent together.
Yet she hardly makes a sound.
Yes, she hardly makes a sound.

She wears a shiny scarlet coat,
Which, repels the weather.
The wind, the snow, the rain, the sleet,
Or all of them together.
Her eyes are bright as stars at night.
Shining through fog and gloom.
Yet she hardly makes a sound.
Yes, she hardly makes a sound.

She keeps me safe in day or night,
Long miles we've gone together.
Though summers sun or winters gloom.
She's warmed me on the coldest day,
And cooled me in the hottest noon.
She is of course my car.
Yet she hardly makes a sound.
Yes, she hardly makes a sound.

E Woods

Let's Talk About Weston

Huddled in a small iron bed.
Very wide awake, though our prayers had been said:
Matthew, Mark, Luke and John,
Bless the bed that I lie on...

Our bed - a blanket and a couple of coats,
Snowy white sheets were unknown to us then,
When my sister was seven.
And I was just ten.

'Let's talk about Weston'
One of us would say,
And thus began the story,
Of our lovely special day.

It started with packed sandwiches,
A bucket and a spade,
The station, the looking forward
To the sand and the penny arcade.

Then the moment we'd all waited for.
The train roaring in so fast,
The rush for the empty carriages.
When its wheels slowed down at last.

And there was a special window seat.
That must have been sent for us.
Then the guard's flag waved, the whistle blew.
This was better than the bus.

The cows, the fields, the meadows,
What memories, what bliss,
Till a sleepy voice said 'I'm tired now,
Goodnight and God bless sis'.

Vee Smith

Possession

I have stood for centuries at the foot of this hill. No sound,
No movement. Just the need to be still. Buds opened, shrank,
fell, rotted in the ground. There were voices in the distance,
but no other sound.

A game of truth rolled in my head, over the pebbles, over the
lead. And if I found the answer I could not have said. I did
not pay attention to any of these things - transient moments,
empty flings. All that I heard was the ocean's wail. The sea
is your prison, its waters my grail. You paid it in full, the
unforeseen debt. I will collect on the insurance yet.

Meantime, this heart wallows deep in grief, thick with hatred
for the ocean thief. Red blood splattered on a rocky wall the
entry pass to this ghostly hall.

I uncovered more than your last speech hid, then I believed in
you more than you did. While you lived I had the capacity for
thought. Without you it signifies less than nought.

Your private things are sacred no more - I threw them at the
man who came begging at the door. In one swift movement every
article removed, but nothing was achieved, nothing was proved.

Now that it is impossible I find I think of things, like
wedding and children - all that time brings. If I could bring
you the gift of life, would I remain your mistress or would
you make me your wife ? Time repeated would
mean more somehow. It would all last longer, less fleeting the
show. A week, a month , a year to go, if I had known then what
now I know.

Can a band of gold really mean that much? Like some modern day Midas with the magic touch. Papers, oaths, ceremonies and words. Binding religion to govern the herds. Such multitudes for the heavenly host, newly converted to the holy ghost. My faith is older than these four church walls. It walked on soil where now there are halls. Pagan priestesses and starlit rites, druids and mystics and ancient insight. These are the truths that I believe, but strong as they are they can not retrieve that life lost on a storm-wrecked night when gales ripped the shoreline and the victim was life.

If you were here now would you seal my hand with the hated and longed for golden band ? Instead I am left with the life that we led, consigned to memory and an empty bed. These are the things that run in my head.

S L Cavers

Reprieve

Distant sounds of gentle purring,
Crescendo now to fearful whirring,
Hear those engines as they loudly roar!
Madly 'cross the sky a-chasing,
Weaving vapour trails like lacing.
Steers a craft we've never seen before.

Through the cumulus white clouds sliding,
Down towards the Earth's crust gliding,
Piercing, like a dart, Earth's atmosphere.
A minute speck when first in vision,
Now we wonder, 'What's its mission?'
Standing watching, petrified with fear.

Faster than the wind it's speeding,
Long and sharp antennae leading,
Like some insect seeking out its prey.
Polished hulk like mirrors shining,
Glistening shape with smooth streamlining,
Manoeuvring like a silver-fish at play.

Children, men and women crying,
Thoughts of war, of grief and dying,
Caused by this machine from Outer Space.
People hope to go on living,
Heavenward, supplication giving,
'Don't obliterate our human race.'

Suddenly it stops its diving,
As quickly as it was arriving,
So it screeches, turns and soars to go.
There's an end to man's foreboding,
With the sound of loud exploding,
End of spaceship! Farewell U.F.O.

C W Foord

The Old Chalice

Many voices have responded amen,
Many sips taken from the cupped rim
Drinking the contents therefrom.

Many lips have given the welcome kiss,
And hearts experienced homecoming bliss,
But have also felt the departing stress.

Many wines have filled the cup,
To be emptied to the very last drop,
Yet, the timeless sap still rises up.

Many faiths have been declared,
In the simple act expressed,
Humbly have come, likewise have left.

The hallowed chalice : the outward expression
For many grateful thanks once given,
On the restoration of a deposed living;
In a past time of deep division.

The thought was the silversmith's to make,
To mould and to shape,
And last while others care and appreciate.

A spirit of creation was then at work
During the labour undertaken;
The spark of genius in the task.

Only now brought out for special occasions,
It's venerated used has spanned the generations,
To hold, and be of itself a treasure trove.

It is kept polished and always shines,
Plated by the caress of folk of all kinds,
But one common belief in their minds.

To take the vessel and to use,
Is a glove-like extension of the hand,
So comfortable and reassuring to dispose;
An honour and pride to be of a continuous band.

There, together, at the altar stood,
Craft and time, wine and blood,
Are in a moment all enshrined.

Eric Ashwell

A Fabulous Pirate

I am a pirate brave and bold,
And so I'll stay until I'm old.
Under the great black flag we fly,
The skull and crossbones makes strong men cry.
And when our ship it hoves in sight
Men all surrender without a fight.

When our ship arrives in port
We tell the tales of battles fought:
Sometimes with telling our tales improve
And ladies listen with looks of love,
Comparing us with men at home
Wanting with us the sea to roam.

We only rob the rich and weak
But never harm the poor and meek,
Though sailors all they flee from me,
When we catch them they bend the knee
In homage to our fearsome crew....
If you're not careful we'll catch you too.

S Taylor

The Cotton Fields

I wanted to see more things
enjoy a different smiles
wake up in different beds
and let new experiences feed my mind.

I had seen the birds flying among the clouds
reaching the sun without looking back at the ground.
I wanted to extend my wings
ascend slowly and once up there enjoy the bliss.

My crystal dreams shattered in one hundred tiny pieces.
The wind started blowing, pushing them towards the sky.
I took a plane carrying a suitcase full of kisses
and said goodbye without faking my smile.

The man-made bird broke free
and my heart started beating faster.
My closed eyes showed me an open field.
The infinity much closer.
Life itself would be my master.

Diego Martinez-Montano

Withered Ramblings

Melancholy silence of fire put to rest.
A road lost forever in a life that's lost its zest
To find inside the beings lost
Is to finally face the cost
And that in all too far to go
In the tears and streams of woe

Some things better left unsaid will yet too soon be here
And in the darkness somewhere you'll finally face your fear
Shadowed ways to places cold
The depth you somehow sold
Like children lost and wandering
The fate, in trance, we chose to bring

Beauty shadowed right and left by deaths almighty head
And music slow and solemn as laboriously we tread
Winters touch beneath the skin
In a race you cannot win
Night angels lost in solitude
With violent graces crude

So now the light begins to fade and the curtains cross the sun
The end is there on muddied paths and nowhere now to run
Oblivion reigns in icy pools
And numbness breaks the rules
Good love, if you could only see
The way we wanted this to be

A Weaver

To Catch A Star

Breakfast TV witters the news,
Letters clunk onto the mat,
The gas fire hisses,
And the wind finds gaps to pour icy draughts
While I play with words in my head.

They spin like stars priceless gems,
Bright and out of reach.
I whirl around with my net
Catching the brightest,
Placing them carefully in my bag.

I look later, only to find dull pebbles, heavy and worn.
I throw them back, and return to my world.

G Cubitt

Thread Bear

He really had nothing
not even stuffing,
just saggy arms hanging loose.
He dangled so badly.
I looked at him sadly
and thought poor old chap, what's the use?

He'd been Granny's treasure
and giving such pleasure
it seemed sad his life had to end.
I picked him up gently.
He didn't resent me.
I'm sure that he said 'Thank you friend'.

Then as I sat sewing
I'm sure he smiled knowing
at last he had regained self worth.
With someone so willing
to get back his filling
I watched with great pride his rebirth.

Like a gourmet indulging
with stomach now bulging.
A bear in a million I think.
I hugged him and squeezed him
and that really pleased him.
I'm certain he gave me a wink.

John Christopher

Men Of War

Tripping senseless
He dives and bruises.
Shudders in fear
And relief alike.

The land lit up
With flares
and striffing bullets.

Soldiers run
like scurrying rats.
Mudfilled trenches
Swallow their boots.

Sandbags piled
As high as heaven.
Their aching backs
given over.

Tired and hungry
They crawl into
their dens.
Sip rum and sleep
like babies.

With pictures
of their wives
and children
Held tight in their hands.

Saiqa Hussain

Ocean

Gigantic, deep blue Atlantic
A bed of foaming tide
Rolling from side to side
A ferocious tyrant
When shakened, awakened
by winds that provoke
and stoke his anger
Causing him to shout
Prance about
like a raving lunatic
Lashing and trashing
anything in his path
Devoid of heart
He lets rip, at boat and ship
Like some hydra-headed monster
from the watery deep, deprived of sleep
causing fear, causing harm
one minute he is angry
The next, so peaceful and calm

L King

Trend

Under the guidance of a trendy vicar
This church is now much freer, brighter, slicker;
Twanging guitars and romping in the aisles.
The vicar is delighted, wreathed in smiles.
A pleasant, beaming, well-intentioned man–
'We bring them back to God as best we can.
It's not a truly reverential age.
More relevant to Youth, this latest stage.
No knells of doom, no threats of vengeful Fate!
Just things to which the youngsters can relate.'
This church, we thought, was meant to offer calm.

A tranquil haven from the world's alarm,
With everything harmoniously designed
To soothe the sprit and delight the mind.
Medieval vestments, brilliant jewelled glass;
The lectern's eagle wings of burnished brass;
Stone tracery as delicate as lace;
The skills of centuries that built the place;
The sermon and the hymns, the prayers, the Creed;
Devout obedience to the parson's lead.

This vicar says, 'The young won't wear that now.
Humility's a thing they don't allow.
I can't stand high above them any more,
Pontificating, laying down the law,
With them below, responding, in the pews.
I have to mingle, entertain, amuse.
Old ritual would drive them up the wall.
The great thing is to get them here at all.'
We said we understood and wished him well.
Do good intentions pave the road to hell?

    G Cox

Zodiac

O, Mr Obconicus what have you done for me?
I thought I was a Libran, now a Virgo I must be.
All this time you've been hiding, up in the sky,
Now at last you've shown yourself- why were you so shy?

Think of all those astrologers working at their charts,
Based upon the principle the zodiac's in twelve parts,
It's easier to divide by twelve and not thirteen-
Why complicate the system? Keep what's always been.

I'll still read the horoscopes for Libra in the press
Though I don't take them seriously, and think they only guess
At what might happen using trends- just a bit of fun-
I'll keep a balanced outlook - cool Virgo I will shun.

J Reeve

Paint Work

Van Gogh I love that man who paints the fields!
I see him lift his brush from which the colour yields-
To make a sudden splash of gold across a canvas bare and cold!
And then a blaze of crimson, deftly places,
Brings to life a swathe of glowing poppies, boldly traced!

The breeze is warm - the air is still-
No time can change this man of skill;
To me he lives - I clasp the gifts he gives;
I'm by his side, to share his tortured soul with pride;
To have his halo touch my life- to shelter me from wounding strife...

Who can doubt the strength that is still there?
Decades have melted to a year,
When skies above his drifting corn
Are rent with clouds- like thoughts all torn,
To gather, gray - a rain of tears; can these wash away his fears?

When driven by his captured mind,
He traps the sun to bless mankind
Who's toils are irksome - laden - weighted,
Often wearied - lost - betrayed;
They long for light but alive in shade.

Cloaked by fate's dark shadow, there seems no worth beyond the callow,
When a simple picture, framed half hidden as if blamed
for being too bright behind a window without light!
Halts a passer-by, who, with turn of head- a glance-
Beholds a miracle 'A harvest field in France....!'

Now seen with eyes dulled by mirrored lies,
With hooded lids- so shamed, so closed-
Dares, with cautious lift, to open wide with urgent question posed;
What is this uncharted promised land?
A bible ? A hoax by painters hand?

But no its the truth the world seems bright the sky's alight
Let sadness go
From Van Gogh's palette love will flow
To cast eternal hope to grow !
His work is done.... The passer-by has just begun!

   D Payn Le Sueur Warner

A Grain Of Light

The shadows are coming
And when they come,
They will not leave.
Everything, they will conquer
Or destroy.
Everything, they will lay waste.

And look!
Set amid the darkness
A grain of light penetrates.
Hope I'd not gone.
Although embraced by darkness
The light is not extinguished,
Instead grows stronger
Despite the odds
And grows to a fire great.

For love is that light
And hope is its strength
Faith its knowledge
And its wisdom is courage.
So that even in fear
It will ever fight the darkness
And rid its slaves of ignorance.

The light gets stronger
And ever brighter.
Amid that darkness,
That light is in you.

Richard Cassidy

Evening

Pink tinged sky of the evening, with the promise
of the future day. Warm and bright around the
setting sun, flowers close their petals in
anticipation of the sun tomorrow.

Dark velvet fingers run across the clouds
encroaching on the day, and darker with
intensity to cover the light, twilight's
colours deepen, red and orange near
the setting sun.

It has taken itself to bed for another
day, black is the night now, but light
from the twinkling stars peep from their
places in God's night, children asleep.
dreaming of pleasures and of tomorrow.

Carrie Snow

First Snow Of Winter

Confetti flakes of purest white
Fluttering softly through the night

The many pointed stars so bright
Silently tumbling in their flight

All of the brother-sister flakes
Are drifting into snow-white lakes

Each one is different it is said
While falling to its earthly bed

Yet they form a seamless curtain
Covering all defects that's certain

A silent blanket on the land
And I wake up in wonderland.

Janis Robertson

Rehearsal

This life is not a rehearsal,
you don't get a second chance,
take all the happiness,
that comes along your way.

If you take the wrong path,
learn as you go along,
you may walk the right path,
if you don't it's not the end.

Don't let happiness pass you,
grip as hard as you can,
remember it's not a rehearsal,
and you don't get a second chance.

Live every day to the full,
and never have any regrets,
the stage is set and you have a part,
to star in your own life.

When your life is over,
and your curtain falls
and you can look back on,
the happiness it's brought.

Angela Wellings

Time Peace

A simple watch upon your wrist
but leave it off and it is missed
you know it's off - but you've glanced
to where your wrist should be enhanced.
To be without it, causes grief
and long to wear it for relief
you are obsessed about the time,
waiting for church bells to chime.
Asking others through the day
'Five minute's later...!' they just say
all through the day you feel so bare
and will not rest, until its there.
You're irritant and need to know
why this day is going slow.
But, once it's on and you feel dressed,
suddenly, you're not obsessed.
Although time goes at the same speed
to glance down, you feel no need
then someone will ask you the time,
you act as if it were a crime.

Geoff Durham

Listening To Landini

His music, with archaic chords.
Old records bears their just rewards.
Rejected by our modern hoards,
what was addressed to ladies, lords.
Instrumental, some, with words.

Landini, died so long ago?
Left priceless beauty which does show;
performed by group, with one 'munrow',
who modern day-no longer know!

Such works are short! Too quickly said;
while I, justify for daily bread, in my stead,
with words, that too, are quickly shed;
my mind, relaxed: and so to bed!

Brian Stevens

Audition Dance

Among their faces I
saw the smack and
thistle of pain as
they turned terpsichorean spin

Wheeling and wracked on
An anchored ankle stage-
struck and bucking back
For mummy who paid

The fees but whose
Barnacle cage holds land-
Locked and dry the
True spit and spirit

Of the thighed and
sighed true dancer whose
only conquering came with
The belly-dancing birth.

    M Whitecross

From London To Liverpool

Swarms of people desperate to board the train,
Pouring into bulging carriages.
Noise smells, tannoy system, mingled bodies,
Business people, students, harassed parents with bewildered children.
I sat snug and smug in my tatty seat with a table.

Train heaves its way out of Euston and onwards, upwards.
As the carriages release their load at each and every station,
The lightened train speeds up, onwards, upwards.
Little villages, countryside, meandering streams, fields.
A magazine to read, the crosswords to complete.

Train lurches into Birmingham and puts on more weight.
Doors spring open, desperate people dash towards spare seats.
I snuggle deeper into my chair and felt content.
The train stumbles and chugs towards Wolverhampton.
Like a never ending barn dance, people stand, move, sit down.
New partners every few stations but I sit in my own little world,
An onlooker of drama that performs between platforms.
The reunions, the farewells, the frustrations and the relief
I feel for each and every one as I am transported onwards and upwards.

Cheshire countryside then houses and gardens and Runcorn's industry.
I shuffle my pocket until I turn up my ticket.
Replacing it I feel reassurance of house keys.
Into Merseyside the train sprints its last lap.
The watery sun sinks low creating a half silhouette of the cathedral.

Edge lane is the dramatic prologue.
I button myself into my coat and tuck a scarf tightly around me.
Bag, completed crossword, suitcase.
We entered the tunnel and the heart soars, onwards and upwards.
Closing to a dramatic finale at Lime Street.
I step out and greet the frosty, crisp air.
My keys jangle an applaud as I walk towards my destination.

Michellejoy Hughes

Animal Adventure

I sat on a rock with a python
and soaked up all the sun
then laughed with the hyena
over something funny he'd done
a gnu told me some stories
the best I've ever heard
then I took down some shorthand
with a secretary bird
I played cards with a cheetah
he won a game of course
I swam in a deep long river
with a giant river horse
I saw a leopard hiding
in the shade of a leafy tree
The elephant quickly spotted her
and called her in for tea
I saw an impala dancing
just by herself in the moon
she was asked if she'd like company
by a very well mannered baboon
I said goodnight to a zebra
My pyjamas striped just like him
I read the monkeys a bedtime story
then one by one tucked them in.

Hazel Houldey

The Stones

Black forests of Britain dripped rain
tears of despair,
Bent branches dipped to the earth,
Unrequited love.

Large stones huddled together,
Whisperers,
A slender stone stood apart,
A beautiful woman.

A majestic stone stared ahead,
A handsome king,
Lesser stones gathered in groups,
A silent Army.

Whisperers huddled together,
Large stones,
A beautiful woman stood apart,
A slender stone.

A handsome kind stared ahead,
A majestic stone,
A silent army gathered together in groups,
Lesser stones.

'Love me' said the woman,
'And I give you Britain'
'A precious stone'
'My love for you,' he mocked,
'Is akin to the hatred of witches.'

'Your hatred' cried the woman,
'Has rejected the love of an angel,
You and your army shall be,' she wept,
'Like your heart of stone.'

So changed the king staring ahead,
A majestic stone,
So changed the silent army,
Lesser stones gathered in groups.

So changed the whisperers,
Large stones huddled together,
So changed the despairing angel,
A slender stone standing apart.

Victoria Helen Turner

Dream

Away from man, away from mankind.
To a land that only exists in the mind.
To a land where you roam unhindered and free.
To a land where you need no daylight to see.
To a land where you need not give answers to questions.
To a land where there's no need to prove that you're special.
Where all are forgiven, where there's no need to pray.
Where there's no money to entice the weak to stray.
No bottled up worries, no cork to explode.
No fear of attack from the young or the old.
If this land where to rise and conquer all souls.
Who would resist ? Nobody knows.

A R Frape

Acronychal Gloom

Dark trees are limned on sombre sky,
The purpling hills presage the night,
And lonely gull, with mournful cry,
Bemoans the passing of day's light.

Stark shadows slowly shuffle nigh,
And pall of smoke shrouds overhead;
Dying wind suspires with final sigh,
Inexorably day is dead.

A chiaroscuro moon peers down,
With scarce appreciable rays,
And here and there around the town
Dim beams attempt to pierce the haze.

Alasdair Maciver

My Magnolia Bush

My magnolia bush is like a fairy tree
with waxen buds
like candle cones
I have no words
that can describe
its incandescent glow,
like porcelain ware
or china rare
one does not dare
to touch the fragile flowers,
and shudder when the cold wind blows
around this sweet creation.
Alas its hour is all too brief
and the driven whiteness of its shining blooms
will fade away, curl and droop
and drop into brown decay
turning the joy it bought into gloom
and in my heart
a dismal sadness and strange grief..........

Ruth Kennedy

It's All In The Game

I see life as a game of cards, and often the deck is stacked high
We are each dealt a hand that we don't understand
With the joker always nearby
But when the odds are against us, and clouds appear in the sky
In comes the sparkle of diamonds, with the brilliance of hope on high
When we need reassurance, and need to know of love
Crimson hearts bring comfort, beating like the wings of a dove

We join several clubs to meet a friend and use spades to dig our plot
Remembering it's all a gamble, making the best of what we've got
The knave, we'll call him jack the lad reminds us good times we've had
And royals always will reign supreme
The imposing king, the stately queen
But it's the dealer who holds the Ace, he knows he stands to gain he shuffles the pack hands out the cards
and gathers them in again.

P D Hollington

The Unicorn

A unicorn came to me last night
While I was lost in mists of dreams;
He was bathed in soft golden light
And spoke to me of legendary times.
We spoke of the queens and kings
Who ruled over long forgotten lands;
We spoke of vanquished witches and rings
With mystical powers not meant for man.
And as we talked so we moved
Through the mists of times, not dreams.
So the unicorn to me did prove
That the old legends live on.
In one night the unicorn came
And spoke to me of the legends;
Of wizards with long forgotten names,
Of himself; and myself too.

J E Alban

Jesus Was . . .

In the coldest months of winter
That come just once a year.
A time of fun and laughter
A time with plenty of cheer.

Christmas isn't joyous for everyone,
Lest we forget the saddened few.
With nothing, starving in a modern world,
You sit back just glad it's not you.

What does Christmas mean?
Do our children remember what for?
Do we ever tell them ?
Or have we closed our door.

A lesson was learned a long time ago
In a story related through the ages.
Of how Jesus came to the Virgin Mary,
It was the start of many stages.

Of the life of a man who was wonderful,
Through his father he created,
Many miracles for many people,
Though his work was understated.

Like the modern we live in
Back then he seemed a threat.
Society didn't understand him,
To them he was just a Jesuit.

So they passed a sentence of death
And marched him through the streets.
With a great wooden cross upon his back,
On a hill he was nailed by his hands and feet.

See how history created this celebration,
And we all, we all take our part.
But the truth must be remembered
In our nations hearts.

When you wake up on Christmas morning
Just sit back and say a prayer.
For a man who lived a long time ago
A man who really cared.

Christmas is a special time
In the coldest months of the year.
It should be treated with respect,
Because that man isn't here.

R C Thompson

One From The Heart

I looked at him on my wall,
His gaze follows me around the room,
His staring eyes so caring and so kind
His smile, if only it were mine,
His face, oh his face as a whole
Reminds me of the sun,
Those colours set off feelings inside
Of which no-one can describe,
If only I could reach out and touch that comforting flesh,
If only he could hear my sweet words
The ones I tell him every night,
If only, if only it were not a dream I dream every night.

Debbie Boyt

The Sea

Swish, swish along the shore,
The endless waves roll in;
The seagull calling out for more
Paddles on the rim;

Crash, crash against the crag
The sea is angry now;
The fulmar, cormorant and shag
Huddle from the wind;

Hush, hush now all is still;
The storm is over now;
The sun goes down behind the hill,
As night begins to fall

Christine M Matthews

The Hands Of Time

A screech of brakes, and burning rubber,
The fumes rise from the ground,
But this is just the start of things,
Then I hear the sounds . . .

The tangled metal, twisting round,
Slicing through the air,
Shattering glass, and crunching bones,
The pungent smell of singeing hair.

All around as people slow,
Hazard lights go on,
The radios continue to play,
The ever background song.

Now the timescale seems to stop,
A second lasts an hour,
As tangled metal starts to breathe,
So flames do now devour.

But flames are soon extinguished,
People sit in shock,
Still time plays its part,
The slowly ticking clock.

When all the debris has been cleared,
The memory remains,
These are the things that never die,
Constantly reliving people's pain.

    P Harvi

Unwritten Rules

The sea whispers out a small subtle breeze
The sun lights the waves with enchantment and ease
The surf that boils out on the smooth sunny floor
A receding liquid moving with unchangeable law
A seagull coping with whatever the tide brings
To us it just shrieks, to Mother Nature it sings
The principles of the sea cannot be adjusted, or ruled
The tides of the earth which can never be fooled
Basic understandings of life look us in the face
From the moon to the sun, every minute little place
Governed by rules that a greater power has written
To be used as our soul strings, to our hearts never smitten
This is just one simple place with just one simple way
Each playing their part of what becomes of the day.

P Larner

Angling Comrades

These are angling comrades at the gare I know
Mick and Colin and two called Joe
Harry and Carl, David and Paul
Terry and Dave, but that's not all
Oz and Steve and Tony's a big guy
If I said, put a worm on your hook, he'd die
Jeanette, also Kevin, he smokes Castella
Sandals on his feet, but he's a nice fella
Nev's dog, Tilley, I hope she doesn't like toffee
She always comes and drinks my coffee
Lol, his lurcher and little Jack Russell
It crunches crabs, as if it were a mussel
There's lots more anglers, not named, that's so
But a really good bunch of pals to know
A laugh, a daft crack, that's what it's about
They'll even help you, if your bait runs out
My poem is ended, it's straight from the lip
So thank you, one and all, for your comradeship.

Peter Edward Waines Briggs

Waiting For The Man

I'm waiting for the man I'm feeling kind of low
I'm waiting for the man to make this feeling go
I'm waiting for the man I feel like shit
I'm waiting for the man and I need another hit
I'm waiting for the man to take away this pain

> To take away this pain
> that's driving me insane
> The pain is twisting
> and pulling my insides
> Suddenly
> my lights go out like the tide
> As I sail through the darkness
> chasing the fool
> Find another hit my body calls
> I sit on the deck
> sweat and feel cold
> This is a junkie's story that already has been told
> Ten thousand times before
> by other fallen men
> Our washed-up souls never to be dry again
> Some have been weak
> some have been strong
> But all of us feel as if we do not belong
> *We just drift on and hum our song*

We're waiting for the man and we all feel low
We're waiting for the man to make this feeling go
We're waiting for the man we all feel like shit
We're waiting for the man we need another hit.

Nic Miller

The Desert Song

Spring,
In No Man's Land.
Yet no bird does sing,
This day.
There's only the burst
Of Staccato gunfire,
Armoured predators
Rumble, roam.
Whilst mad dervish storms
Raise whorls in desert sand
Sands in time's hourglass
Trickle out
Then drift away
On no hope winds
Lean pariah keens
To a surrogate moon.
Even the stars fall down
When the great birds swoop
Which punch home
A lethal message.
Now there is a deathly hush
All has withered away
Lone phoenix hides
In war's ashes.

Terri Fisher

Patient In Mental Home In Travnik

Mad, mad they called us
Locked away from sight.
Far from the normal world
Suffer would they to see our plight.

But it is they who are the crazy ones.
They who rape and kill.
They can't see their actions.
Like us they never will.

The snipers came too close to us,
So we were left alone
Forsaken by our carers
They all fled so soon.

Mad, mad they called us
But not so mad as they.
We own no guns or bitter greed.
And we know how to pray.

Audrey Lay

The Humble Rose

The memorable beauty of the fragrant rose
That lies quite still in sweet repose.
   The scented petals in scarlet red
   Has pride of place in the flower bed.
   Gently swaying in the breeze
      Dwarfed in statue by the apple trees.
      Its place of excellence steeped in tradition
      Will remain supreme in any position.
         Handed down to give great pleasure
      A legacy of love that we must treasure.
This wonderful flower of great distinction
Will live forever an inspiration.

H R Jones

I Think Not Neigh, Astray Stay

Upon my heart the whispers, tales
that cannot neigh express upon any
Cannot neigh tell the world with truth
Sunken Soul remember nights are pretty to each blind
and Fall is ever roaming to each who see
Noth' Mouth I can hear not neigh a sound
A thought from grass's weed

Upon my tears they never show aloud
They whisper and curl the bodies exhaust
Only One raging against me Only one
but to travel to Mars - think not neigh arrive ever home
Thinks one cries and not neigh will hear
Only a passer by the deaf hear one cry

Nothing nout me doubt no can't see
Tell me deep nothing and listening in awe
Why have you brought me here, left
And now inch carry on
Tales of the soul crunch and growl
Smash and think and die with age
Carrots in the sky the shady misty nigh
Think need not neigh another day has sighed

Upon my head are fears climbing on my walls
Leaving one petrified falling from the sky
and wings of hope always swoop by
Always pass me by, pass me by
Hope a heavy contention, love never a hear mention
I not neigh - one should leave astray
But dam reason and care glues astay
Astay Until
Upon my life there's nothing

Anita Branagan

Fat Fool

'Give it to me for I am the happy man'
Sang the fat fool
Such a mouthful
Of unspeakables

The wolf whistle legs of an unspun daughter
Of an unsung son
Family fortune cookies
And then some

'Hey Dad' they drive
'Where is the chicken that has no skin?'
J'ai accuse
(And your excuse?)

The unspun daughter smiles kindly
Upon the unsung son's son
He strokes her neck
Then turns to me
And offers up the sacrificial meat

'Give it to me'
Sang the fat fool

D A Seabright

Love, God, Father Xmas And The Tooth Fairy

It was I who sent the letter-bomb to Santa
(gluttonous patriarch of the festive junta.)
Love, God, Father Xmas and the Tooth Fairy:
emotional scrabble, spiritual racism,
a marketing icon and an infant's sweetener
for the bitter medicine of capitalism.

L O V E . . . we try to fit in and around
the spaces left by others, in quest of
triple word score circumstance and the concealment
of awkward letters (to be deducted from total).
Too often we are left sitting alone
challenging the validity of every word.

God has been deemed 'not economically viable'
since the introduction of miracle related pay
so while Christmas Day reminds us
of our lack of faith and Easter to atone,
Valentine's Day reminds us that we are all alone.

Every day must be made to seem special in some way
because an optimistic consumer
is a consuming consumer
and the corporate culture vulture preys on sentiment.

So dear Father of the pissed masses
I turned the corpse of the old year over,
it was maggot ridden and putrid
but then I always knew it . . .
who would believe me?

The bullet is already
in society's head
and is working its way
to the heart.

Stephen Dulson

The Witch's Spell

Hubble, bubble,
Rot and rubble,
Crime and torture,
Blind man's stubble
In the cauldron,
Boil and bake,
Pace of slug and blood of snake,
Tiger's pounce and spider's quake,
For 20 hours,
Poke with stake,
Panther's growl
40 knives,
Young wolf's howl,
And cat's nine lives.
Nose of guppy
Tail of rat
Death to kindness,
In seconds flat.
Let it bubble in the pot,
Turn up heat
Till burning hot,
Will turn green
For all
To see
For 30 minutes,
Menacingly!
Yellow, purple,
Blue and white
In the cauldron al the night.
The child's flesh, skin and bone,
Will then transform,
To rock
And stone.

Let this spell be cast,
And last,
Until 1000 years have past.
Hubble, bubble,
Rot and rubble,
Crime and torture,
Blind man's stubble!

Duncan Cook (8)

Little Witch

Little witch of the morning,
Black as darkest night;
Baby Bast from Egypt,
Watching the swallows' flight.

Little witch of the shadows,
Eyes of emerald green;
What stories you could tell me
Of the wonders you have seen.

Little witch of sable,
How much do you know?
Have you heard the singing
In the desert winds that blow?

Little witch, the black cat,
Born of the Blue Nile's song;
Can you hear the river
Meandering along?

Little witch of moonbeams,
Watching a falling star;
Can you hear your Mother
Calling from afar?

Little witch of starshine,
Looking to the sky;
Hear your distant drummer
Play Egypt's lullaby.

Trudy Pickering

Verduna

Beyond beyond, there is a world:
Verduna is her name.
Within our realm,
Yet in another universe,
She basks in sunshine from an orange sun.
No arctic wastes to chill her temperate clime,
Just leagues and leagues of sub-tropical paradise,
And equatorial desert plains.
Like Earth she is a world of azure blue,
Her sweeping oceans teeming to the brim with life.
She has no seasons: summer all year long,
Her jagged mountains draped with endless trees.
Those crags that overshadow parkland plains:
A verdant shrubbery decked with flowers of every hue,
Attended by clouds of butterflies,
By flocks of colourful songbirds,
And giant stingless bees!
This tangled undergrowth gives way
To juicy grasslands green.
The people on this planet - coloured orange -
Are children of the sun:
Blessed with being immortal,
To play, so free, with clawless cougars, on lawns
And lazy beaches lined by sentinel palms.
Look! See them riding the backs of giant bees!
Come join us here in their home village -
Helletrius - in Qualaduxa: A Middasian land -
A place with history
That time forgot;
Where you can come
And join in all the fun:
Verduna!

Paul Butters

Fright

They always do too much in those films,
Lay the horror on with a trowel:
Spring hideous spooks from cupboards,
Show a creature whose face is . . . a towel;
Build up suspense with discordant chords,
Punctuated with screams of the damned
As hanging corpses are sliced with swords
And the gates of Hell loudly slammed.

But horror, for me, is a subtler thing -
A non-smoking family, home late,
Catch the whiff of a recently burnt cigarette,
See the stub of one left on a plate.
(So who - worse, *where* now - is the smoker?
They huddle protectively -
One foolishly picks up the poker -
Imagining what they will see.)

Or you stand on a Cornish headland, just you,
Watch the glorious summer sun sink . . .
And hear the tiniest cough (a-hyou, hyou!)
'But there's no-one . . . ! What the hell?' You think
As the cough is repeated (a-hyou, hyou!)

You leave the headland, hurry away
Push the nagging cough from your mind;
Then on the road, in the fading day,
You're aware of *footsteps* behind.

You turn, and of course there's no-one there.
Some echo or aural trick?
Just a couple more hundred yards to the house,
So make a run for it, quick!

No need for those mega-horror films.
Feet following can set me off,
Or cigarette smoke in an empty house,
Or a small . . . persistent . . . disembodied cough.

Adrian Vale

Bluebell Wood

There were fairies living in the dell
Down in Bluebell Wood,
We saw them weave their magic,
We were very quiet and very good.

They wore colours bright as rainbows
Their gossamer wings would glow bright,
We saw them dance and sing sweet songs
Watched them prance in sheer delight.

Fairy dust sprinkled on butterfly wings
Sparkled and dazzled as colours grew,
Then a myriad of glorious butterflies
Raised their wings to the sun and flew.

Their gentle, musical laughter so clear,
Filled the dell as again magic adorned -
The fairy dust, sparkling brilliant blue,
And a wondrous garden of bluebells was born.

We knew they saw our presence,
Their smiles told us, - you're okay,
And we know we were truly blessed
That they trusted us children that day.

Sometimes I open the secret gate
To the memory box in my mind,
The enchantment of Bluebell Wood lives on,
Stored and remembered throughout time.

Margaret Dominey

Merriment And Mirth

Mixed up magic moments of merriment and mirth,
Pals of mine in pantomime, it's the greatest show on Earth.
We gather at the club each Sunday, for pints and games of cards,
The merriment is genuine, it never is charades.

Mixed up magic moments, wry comments with repartee,
When it's past, the wag will ask 'Who said that: was it me?'
The answer is resounding: 'Play your cards you fool!'
'He needs that ace.'- 'Just look at his face, and he's falling off his stool.'

Mixed up magic moments of friendship, trust and truth,
Of cards and laughs at photographs, of 'Al' in his birthday suit.
So come on my kind of people, 'That's Dennis, I've quoted him,'
Let's keep the game always the same, but can you cut the din?

Mixed up magic moments when the cleaner enters the room;
· She'll ask, 'What's this! You're all still here, are you going home soon?'
Slick answers coming from all directions, she empties ashtrays fast,
Then she hurries to sort another room, and returns at quarter past.

Stephen L Rogers

In Praise Of Gorse

Be still my soul and listen
To the gorse that relieves me from remorse
It pops its seed and propagates
Carried by the wind at any rate
It increases and multiplies and fills the earth
It must have ears for it hears God's word.

It's not the lily and yet it's quite splendid
The bees nestle in its golden petals
To extract the nectar and convert to honey
For natural cure and to make life sunny.
As the morning dew glistens and the air with sweet scent
is filled, the songsters all around are duly thrilled.

Like all things wild it is but a child
And needs protection from wanton wiles,
To flint and match it is but tinder
To inflame the skies and reduce to cinder.
Its dark brown bones remind us wholly
'Dust thou art to dust returnest was not spoken of the soul'.

Mary Ryder

Say Cheese!

A smile can bring out the feeling,
Of a hope beyond belief.
It sparkles like the sunshine,
Gentle as a raindrop on a leaf,
It's a way to communicate,
Without the need for words,
It can almost be angelic,
Like daybreak singing from the birds.
It makes you want to sing and dance,
When someone smiles at you,
It's innocently infectious,
Brings out a smile from you.
Said to be an exercise,
To strengthen all the face,
Effortlessly it grabs you,
No need to win the race.
Out walking in the sunshine,
On a hazy summer's day,
Just take a look and see,
At all the smiles, that come your way.
It can almost make you dizzy,
As your heart leaps up with joy,
The way you do it all depends,
Serious, happy, coy,
A smile comes from the heart,
It stays with you all the while,
So take a look around you,
Go on, why don't you smile!

Tracy Heaton

Something!

Better sleep tightly tonight, my dear,
Not least if you value your skin,
Close all the windows and lock all the doors,
Else something out there might drop in . . .

Beware of the full moon rising,
Where'er in this world you may be,
'Twould be very unwise
Should you open your eyes,
E'er the bogeyman drops in for tea!

Look under the bed tonight, my dear,
Check the wardrobe and cubby hole, too,
Fasten the curtains and pull down the blind,
Else something starts looking for you . . .

Care not for the wriggling spider,
Where'er in this world you may be,
'Twould be sad so I fear
Should one tickle your ear,
After crawling right up from your knee!

Tuck in the covers tonight, my dear
And pull them right up to your chin,
Grab hold of teddy and snuggle him tight,
Chance something in black wander in . . .

Steer clear of the cross-eyed moggie,
Where'er in this world you may be,
'Twould be sad if fate deems
You to suffer bad dreams,
As the witches familiar roams free!

Pray cover your face tonight, my dear,
And stuff cotton wool in your ears,
Hush up your breathing and try not to shake,
Less something out there stirs your fears . . .

Spurn the soft whispers of darkness,
Where'er in this world you may be,
'Twould be fatefully crass
If it came thus to pass,
That dark voices drove you out your tree!

D Gregson

Blind

I drink through the night rejecting love
My head feels light, I'm blind and drunk
Can't see Your face, though You're here by my side
Can't hear Your voice, calling to me through the night
I always push You out of my sight

I'm standing here in the arms of a stranger
Looking for love, finding danger
With frozen lips and a stone cold heart
Countless kisses for a moment then I part
Running off, into the dark.

I'm staring outside through the windows of my mind
Seeing only darkness, feels like I'm blind
Outside the rain beats down on the windowpane
Like the tears falling from my eyes again
Feels like my guilt will never end.

As I fall the world keeps turning round
I'm standing alone, in the midst of a crowd
I see people around me, yet I feel alone
And deep down in my soul, I feel so cold
I only want You to call me Your own.

I can't see, for You're invisible to my sight
Yet I know You're not distant, it's me who is blind
It only takes a revelation of Your love to open my eyes
So through the darkness I will run to You
To a love which is right and true
Knowing all I need to do is trust and obey
The love which will enfold my heart, eternally

You know every deed I've done
In my life You see all my wrongs
Yet You'll love me
And never leave me
Like a father to a child.

Andrea Smith

Technology

Technology has been made by man - striving for scientific plans
To make the world a safer place - for us all - or so they say
To have a life with so much ease
Leaving time to do as we please.

But have they perhaps just gone too far
With robotic this and robotic cars
Computers that can do all sorts
What are these mega bites really for
A machine with a memory it's quite absurd
But will they one day take over earth.

Machine replacing the labour of man
Taking over wherever they can
Offices no longer alive with chatter
Only machinery that doesn't even clatter
Progressing to a scientific dream
But are these things all that they seem.

Robot computers someday in our homes
Taking over - almost like clones
They'll tackle even the most difficult task
And we'll sit back - no questions to ask
As they slowly take over in life's everyday chores
And when will they realise they need man no more.

Machines that now walk and talk with great skill
With programmes that no human mind could fulfil
From factory lines to nuclear stations
Controlling banking within our nation
Almost human in kind - when in control
But never forget that they have no soul.

Does it perhaps sound unlikely to you
That machines could control the things that we do
Or take over our very existence
Like some kind of movie you've watched from a distance
That perhaps left you with an odd kind of chill
How easily machines can be programmed to kill.

These so-called computers - controlled by man
But somewhere in secret there must be a plan
To enable machines to programme themselves
Can you possible imagine that kind of hell
When man would be fighting alone to survive
And machines would control if you live or you die.

Irene Sutherland

In Praise Of Books

They've brought the world into my home
Words on printed page.
Between the covers of a book
I see through every age.
Through them I've travelled far and wide,
In far-off foreign lands.
On snow-capped mountain tops I've stood.
Or rode on desert sands.
I've sailed with Vikings on the seas,
And dived for sunken gold,
Met noble kings and emperors
And warriors of old.
The pages told me many things
Of earth and outer space.
How man set foot upon the moon,
Brought wonder to my face.
I've learned of the wondrous things,
Why we have night and day
And when their nesting time is done
Why swallows fly away.
How games are played and cars are made
The lines have told me so.
What makes the wind blow loud and shrill
And how the palm trees grow.
Since the time that I first heard
A simple word or two,
Books have so enhanced my life,
Old classmates as we grew.
When at last old age will come
Life's story nearly told.
I'll spend it with my special friends
Shelves of leafy gold.

    David Dillon

Ten Words

Sovereignty above division,
Eternal source of clear vision;
The only way that works for all.
Lustral sunshine follows nightfall.

Greatness stems from *humility*,
Enjoy friendship's equality.
Gifted wisdom to meek unfold,
Refining Truth our Oversoul.

Sincerity beyond pretence,
When strife defies our confidence.
Oceans that flow, comets that shine,
Break through clouds veiling earth's design.

The energy of sea and space,
Sharing exalts, self-rule debase.
Future hope, world unity,
Inspires constant *fidelity*.

Loyalty outlasts cleverness,
Caring is love's togetherness.
Happy family, young and old,
With esprit de corps, safe stronghold.

Surmount outrage and tyranny,
Prosper freedom through *equity*.
World assemblies of free nations,
Regenerate right relations.

Joined by crystal-clear *purity*,
Vice outpaced by maturity;
Press on, promote the common good,
Away from hang-ups and falsehood.

Wake to the inward light of truth,
Perish lying in age and youth.
Clear conscience bound to *honesty*,
High duty casts out travesty.

Life is community of love,
Charity, base wrong will remove.
Our neighbour's needs we can but serve,
Befriend the weak without reserve.

Coveting is profanity,
Vast treasure in *tranquillity*.
Peace is in being not having,
True to the light everlasting.

    James Leonard Clough

The Irish Jig

The times of knees and fairy tales have long long since gone by
Often when I think of them I really want to cry
I know we all must older grow, but children on my knee
Was such a very natural thing, why can't it always be?
But life brings compensations now mine have grown so big
They bring me their own tinies, shall I dance and 'Irish Jig'
They've got videos ad computer games, I'm not sure they're very good
But now I've grown to seventy-five, do you really think I should?

A Gillmeister

A Stone's Throw

A stone's throw
The stranger called to Jack
Who had travelled far
From the west on foot
In which direction
Should the stone fall
Asked Jack
To the south
Way down yonder
That a way
He thanked the stranger
And moved on
One half mile
Jack did travel
For the place he seeks
Still no sight there was to be
Jack asked some other
A stranger in the village
How far
It is a stone's throw
The second stranger replied
Just how many stones
Must I need to throw
Before I can reach
The place I seek
Jack asked the third stranger
I do not know I cannot say
How heavy are the stones
You throw to that way
It is to that a way
Across yonder
To a crow's fly
Stone the crows
I've found my way.

Ruth Watts

Machine Metal And Man

I woke that solemn morning, the day we had to part,
The rain it came, each droplet rang, and echoed in my heart.
You robot brother of my life, can you feel the wrench?
Now for me it's time to leave, your cold corroding bench.
They're giving me a handshake, this is our last goodbye,
Machine and man, we've breathed as one, these fifty years or nigh.
Sometimes I grew to hate you, with your never-ending toil,
Yet my blood is intermingled, with your lubricating oil.
I helped and shared your ice cold steel, as you had shared my strife,
And I in humble gratefulness, shared my ice cold life.

Sometimes your power seemed doubled, you drank from me your fill,
You drained from me my hope and tears, you broke my fragile will.
Side by side with rusting brain, our rotting bodies stood,
Friend by friend, or foe by foe, as both searched younger blood.
The only time we separate, the hours I steal to sleep,
Yet the centre of my nightmare, my soul is in your keep.
Metal shavings on the floor, a lifetime's curling dream,
You lifeless hopeless metal giant, you heartless cold machine.

I've fed you by conveyer, I've polished up your brass,
You're only tinged with slight despair, now time has come to pass.
Each shape to cut and file and mould, to bend and twist and turn,
To push and pull, to lift and lay, and feel the blisters burn.
To stack and pile and haul away, each hour they multiply,
Their target must be reached this day, before it's time to die.
As I wear out too late I know to shed my beads of sweat,
Too many years for me to oil, and save my chained regret.

Today I close my grit filled eyes, to shut you from my sight,
I'm trading you for clasping hands, and spoken words polite.
You can share my handshake, you can hear my last goodbye,
Gone the thoughts of times I've wished, that one or both could die.
Will I be left with half a life, and only half a soul?
Half a wish, and half a hope, and only half a goal.
Friend or foe you hunk of steel, your brain preserved in grease,
I think you too are wondering, for which will be relief.

Vera Oxley

Fairies In Summer

Sparkling wings I have,
shining in the sun.
Among the roses I lie,
eating sunflower pie.
I float around gardens
picking petals,
to work my magic
for people that wish.
I fly away.
I will make my magic, another day.

Luke Daniel Gruber Prince (7)

Black Night

The end of my life,
Soon, soon.
The end of the world,
Nuclear determination.
An expanding universe
How many earths?
How many revolving around a sun?
A son of energy, the son of life
My energy, my life.
Man's enemy -
Why man of course
Tales from a comet, beyond the grave?
The after life?
Bones and decay
Death to all!

Ananka Lyall

Sequence

Through our life runs a rugged trail,
We either shine, or else we pale.
Infancy at our mother's breast,
She teaches us, and she knows best.
And as a tiny child we learn,
The love and anchor that we yearn.

Time slips by, and we leave for school,
We fare at study, and the rules.
Progress at college, and take a job
Climbing ladders to make a bob.
I meet a girl with golden hair,
I know that love is in the air.

We wed one day in early spring,
Set up home in an urban ring.
Success, promotion in my job,
I really am a frightful nob!
One day my wife she said to me,
'A father you are going to be.'

The wonder of the role reversed
My wife and I are so immersed.
Our son, she teaches on her knee,
He is the clone that once was me.
Now, that good truth of parenthood,
Is well and truly understood.

I travel to my work each day,
And deal with trials on the way.
My son, he is a juvenile,
We try to guide him all the while.
I love my wife, my wife is fun.
On course through life, and I have won.

Retirement now, it is my way,
We take is easy, day by day.
My wife is frail, my hair is white,
But all through life, was my delight.
We reminisce of times we spent,
Our earthly life to us is lent.

Ann Easton

The Other Word

Shall I write,
To continue this plight,
The poet lay and said,
Shall I fight,
To continue this flight,
Whilst pouring in this bed,
Shall I race,
To a beautiful place,
That's residing in my head,
Shall I face,
The wondrous pace,
That keeps my pleasures fed,
Shall I pertrue,
My love for you,
I call my woman home,
For if I do,
I've still a few,
Words left from this poem,
For there remains a word,
You have not heard,
That deserves my feelings true,
For it can't be read,
Or picture said,
To preserve my youth for you.

Anthony John Ward

The Barrel

Stuck in the barrel, no way out.
People running all around, no point in trying to shout.
The emptiness around, don't hear a sound.
Stuck in the barrel, no way out.

Where are we going? Does anyone really know?
There are barrels all around us, nobody cares to show,
To know, to know. To show, to show.
No need to bother shouting, they don't really want to know.

Clinging for a grip, to stop you slipping down,
But the barrel's pretty slippy all the way down.
The cartridge will stop you, before the hammer's down
But when the hammer hits the pin, you'll be seeing all around.

Out of the barrel, what a way to go,
In a world where the pressure
You don't feel it six below.
In a world where the pressure,
You don't feel it six below.

Tim Davis

The Bookshelves Of Time

Black they are, the towering bookshelves of time
Smooth as ebony, glistening, nursing each precious tome!
Held in protective custody.
Jealous of the gaps,
Reluctant to release, but eager to receive,
The return of missing kin.
No stretch of hand can reach the highest shelves
They fade, far into infinity.
But all knowledge beckons,
Is found,
    Recorded,
        Lost,
            Erased,
                Destroyed,
                    Found again.
    Seek, it's all there.
In the towering bookshelves of time.

Alfred Tubb

Miscarried

You are the one who was not to be
For nature ended your being
Long before your birth was due
And left us bereft of seeing
Our own child to care and love
And guide through childhood days
We mourned you as we lost the joy
Of ever knowing your little ways.

They say you never miss the child
That you have never seen
But I knew you were there within me
And the joy that should have been
For all my long life I have missed you
And wonder of how you would be
If you had been born to be with us
A new name on the family tree.

Is there a place in heaven
For the child who never was born?
And will I go there and meet you
When my presence on earth is gone?
There is one little hope within me
That God took you into His care
And will grant me a joyous blessing
To meet you sometime, somewhere.

Thelma Paolozzi

The Train Is Running Late

The train is running late, *again!*
The train is running late
Calling at this place and that place . . .
. . . but the train is running late
'We apologise for the inconvenience'
But the train is running late
'Passengers on platform two, your train is running late'

There's trouble on the line they say
There's trouble on the line
'So passengers on platform two
Please note, there's trouble on the line'
It can't be leaves, the day is dry
It isn't frost, there's none
It isn't snow or lumps of ice
It's surely *not* the sun?
Ha! They've just announced the reason why
There's trouble on the line
Some sheep escaped along the way -
That's the trouble on the line!

    G Carpenter

Morning Call

'I'm awake! I'm awake!' you can hear me mutter
As I get out of bed all in a fluster.
'Don't make such a row' I call from the door,
While I hunt for my slippers - somewhere on the floor.
The sun is shining as I go down the stairs,
One of those days when my world has no cares.
The noise is louder as I reach the hall
Out in the garden they're having a ball.
Once in the kitchen I get their breakfast,
Perhaps that will keep them quiet at last!
I open the door and head for the lawn
'Do you realise it's only just dawn?'
They gather round the table - each jostling for a place
The din dies down - a smile appears on my face.
'That's better - now please do keep quiet
Or you'll have the neighbours starting a riot
Because some people (who I think are wrong)
Cannot stand an early morning bird song.'

    Margaret Phillips

The Hero

He is a man of many parts,
Of many complexities -
Allowing his alter ego
To dominate his mind.
He has control
But will not acknowledge that.
With his insincere, sincerity
And distorted truth,
He walks a path of many variations
On a theme of pain.

He is the wolf in sheep's clothing,
The rampart sexual hero
Of his fantasies,
Leaving in his wake
A gaggle of giddy worshippers,
Who knew him,
Too briefly to see,
His shortcomings, his feet of clay.
He needs their adulation -
In his escapism,
They are participants.
He sees them in rosy hue,
All blemishes blurred
By the indulgent past.
But when the dreams
Are shattered, for our dark hero
What of his ego then?

She has seen into his prismatic soul,
She can accept its diversity,
She has known this man,
She is his reality.
He is her shining knight.
But when she has gone -
No longer able to tolerate
The double standards of his truth -
How will he cope, with his own reality?
How will he cope, when she has gone?

Hazel Houston Hewitt

Diamond

Diamond
Prismic
Shining bright
Dancing rainbows
Coloured lights
Strong
Define
Deceptive heights
Inward
Ever inward
To the centre of the mind.

Diamond
Reflection
False or true?
Of ever-changing shapes
Delight
Renew
Hypnotic movement
Reaching in
Ever reaching in
To the centre of the mind.

Diamond
Surface sparkling
Upon each turn
On every side
Blossom opening
Expansion wide
Living crystal minds
Look different
But the same.

Diamond
Mystic tales you tell
A thousand facets
To behold
A thousand people listening
But only one
Your secrets will be told
To the centre of your mind.

Jan Duncan

Lost

I'm all alone lost, lost,
Crunching the silver frost.
I'm all alone crying, crying,
Just afraid of dying.
I ran away, away,
When will night become day?
I lie painfully on the ground,
Just waiting to be found.

Emily Victoria Hughes (11)

The Heart Of The Matter

Oh, the mind, it has mountains
And valleys - and troughs of despair;
Moments of madness with nobody there.
Cliffs of unscaleable, shakeable thoughts,
Fields full of battles never been fought.
Oh, the mind, it has secrets
Too deep to be told
Lies, and half-truths left out in the cold;
Stories and fables of times lived and gone,
Times of great deeds and days of great wrong.
The mind makes you brave, courageous and bold
The mind holds your memories when you are old;
Oh, the mind, it has daydreams as high as the sky;
Wishes that once made you laugh, made you cry.
Oh, the mind, is a powerful, masterful toy
No matter whether you're girl or you're boy
Be careful, my friend - 'ere it leads you astray -
Think of tomorrow - but hold on to today.

Elizabeth Mitchell

Voyage To Æaea

I

Gleaming in waterproofs, she walks with me,
my sleek enchantress, changing rain to shine.
(Oh, how her motion thrills me to the spine:
the sight, the sound, a savour of the sea,
her shimmering, rubberised lubricity,
her slinky form and lithe liquescent line,
her tactile lure, - to entice me all combine!)
We kiss. The day draws in; and so does she.

I browse the breathless valley of your breast
(the touch entrancing setting pulses prancing!)
Breathe your warmth from rain-chill proofing pressed
(the sensual piquancy your spell enhancing);
and, (as Priapus rules), responding sighs
reciprocate the rhythm of our thighs.

II

Oh, when she moves, musked in cool macintosh,
and, glistening seaward, slips her arm in mine,
then up to windward points the bowsprit fine!
From bust to boots, her slickering swish and swash
excites a swell quite sets my decks awash.
Her flashing skirts like storm-tossed sea-nymphs sign
the approaches to some Siren-sung shoreline:
So, to her Sanctuary we play and josh.

Exploring promontories and creeks, each shape -
sweet Circe, here my odyssey must cease,
and all my captive seamen crave release! -
My voyaging fingers find your Fairest Cape:
Though I be changed to beast and stricken dumb,
I'll make your Port, for there I needs must come!

Bernard Brown

Consolation Prizes

Seeing a competition for a best garden plot,
I thought it something at which I'd have a shot.
My friends all told me I had fingers green,
Encouraging words for an old 'has been'.
So I sat down and wrote a very long list,
Of seeds I needed, making sure none were missed.
In time they were planted and what a beautiful array,
I felt sure I'd have the best display.
But pride always comes before a fall,
My neighbours cat made an early morning call.
In my best flower bed, his visiting card he left,
My blooms scattered everywhere, I was bereft.
No chance now to win that coveted prize,
There was the evidence before my very eyes.
Then I remembered the Annual Village Fete,
I'd enter for the best vase of flowers before it was too late.
My prize blooms cut, and in crystal vase displayed,
I was delighted with the colourful splash they made.
The judges thought so too, and 2nd prize I won,
Congratulations and praise from everyone.
Don't let life's disappointments cause you to despair,
Often there are consolation prizes waiting for you to share.

E Kathleen Jones

Elevenses And All That

It is a cup; that cup indeed,
    The cup that really cheers;
We start our day, yes, with that cup
    Soon as the sun appears:
A die-hard custom, you'll agree,
    We learned at mother's knee;
But, says tradition, it's a must -
    That precious cup of tea!

Throughout our day a reason's sought,
    That custom to renew;
Elevenses or three o'clock,
    A headache or the flu:
A neighbour calls - or friend from far -
    A pleasure for to see;
But soon, with joy, they'll join us for
    That welcome cup of tea!

In pleasure bent, or sorrow fraught,
    Companion it will be,
It satisfies our yearning thirst
    At ten or half past three;
But come what may, or walk of life,
    Whate'er or who we be,
One thing in common we all share -
    That splendid cup of tea!

Fredk A Hays

Those Little *Fruit*

Grapes
Come in
Funny shapes.
Long or thin
Fat or slim
Oblong or square
And some have hair
Possibly curved, oval or round.
But don't tread on them, they make a funny squishing sound.

David J Pratt

Solo

Driving along in the car
Nobody knows where you are,
Whether going out or home
You are by yourself, alone,
Not a soul gives a fig or a toffee
If you stop for lunch or a coffee,
Take a left or a right turn
Or how much rubber you burn.

There you are the solitary one
Not a living soul under the sun,
In the whole wide universe
Wonders if you want to reverse,
To be part of the human race
Take the kindness from another's face
Warm to someone else's song -
But have I been alone too long?

Marian J Prebble

Hallowe'en

It's midnight and the bells are ringing,
Listen the ghosts and ghouls are singing,
And for an hour till it's day,
The evil things are out to play.

Witches fly upon their brooms,
Haunting bangs in haunted rooms,
Because it's now Hallowe'en night,
Prepare yourself for a nasty fright.

Zombies rise from the dead,
Creep slowly, to your bed,
You wake up to the monstrous stare,
Welcome to your worst nightmare.

Skeletons pour into the street,
Listen to their dancing feet,
But creeping up, nice and slow,
Is the wretched cocks crow.

Hear it now the clock strikes one,
Bringing an end to the evil fun,
They race back to their graves and then,
Wait for Hallowe'en night again.

   Becky Cole

A Shot In The Dark

In a shack by the river where the blue grasses grow
Lives an old gnarled gangster, name of Moonshine Joe
Some recall he was rich in them prohibition days
Ask him for some stories, he'll pick his ear and gaze
Yeah, he had women by the dozen, snapped fingers for his food
Remembering, he smiles, hah, them days were good
There was Black-eyed Frankie, the juggler and big Sioux
The five Riordan sisters to name but a few
At the local Speakeasy where you spoke a little hard
You won the game with the closely hidden card.
There was Li'l Lil with the hourglass silhouette
Whose loving would leave a Sultan in debt
They say she was half dead when Moonshine found her here
At the Palomino Club, then they say that he turned queer
He slammed the suite door whispered 'Admit no one'
Turned the catch on the hidden drawer, felt for his gun
'Gimme a name, Lil he flipped a chip
'Oh honey I love you,' Moonshine burst her lip
She ran from his grasp, had her back against the door
'It was your brother Melvin.' She screamed as she hit the floor.

Jeanette Latta